Common Ground

Whole Language and Phonics Working Together

Priscilla L. Vail

PUBLISHED BY
MODERN LEARNING PRESS
ROSEMONT, NJ

For my daughters and grandchildren,
who keep me up-to-date about
children's books.

With thanks and love,
P.L.V.

ISBN 0-935493-27-1
Copyright 1991© by Priscilla L. Vail
 For information address Modern Learning Press/Programs for Education, Rosemont, NJ 08556. Item #550

Contents

Foreword

Here's an irony. Proponents of both whole language and phonics want children to read and write easily, accurately, and joyfully. Yet language — terminology and labels — is driving many intelligent, benevolent people apart. The ongoing (never-ending?) debate over the teaching of reading and writing has led to confrontations and extreme positions, instead of united action on behalf of our children. How and whether students read and write will have a major impact on all our futures. The goal is too important to be compromised by factionalism. We need to move from rival turf to common ground.

Recent pressures have forced many administrators and teachers to choose EITHER whole language OR phonics. This deprives students of the full range of experiences they need and deserve. When adults go to extremes, kids pay the price. One-sided teaching makes a lop-sided offering.

Waldo Jones, legendary elementary school principal, often says that each school is made of both structure and texture. The same is true of language, and programs for language arts instruction. In language, structure and texture create, and operate within, a symbiosis; interdependent, each nurtures the other, each needs the other for strength, each complements the other. Operating together, they form a handclasp of common purpose, an alliance for literacy, a friendship for children.

Structure refers to the nuts and bolts used in assembling or decoding written language. Multi-sensory phonics instruction provides this solid grounding. Texture refers to the ornamentation which gives language its color, intensity, rhythm, and beauty. Whole language instruction provides texture by soaking children in literature. Structure by itself would be boring, just as free-floating texture would be flimsy.

Structure is a platform for creativity, and through texture language reaches its nobility of purpose.

As structure and texture are mutually enhancing in daily living, they are entirely compatible in the classroom. When offered together, in the common purpose of teaching children to read and write, they open up ever-expanding access to the world of print.

Pie in the sky? No. For the past eighteen years, I have worked with students and teachers in grades k-4, developing, using, and enjoying combinations of materials which offer both structure and texture. This book offers guidelines for those who would like to broaden their base in either category, and shows how the two aspects of the one phenomenon — human language — can work in concert.

Personal teaching experience and observations in classrooms across the country lead me to three fundamental comments on each aspect.

On Structure

1. Knowledge of structure can't reliably be intuited or inferred. Most children need direct, multi-sensory instruction.

2. Direct instruction need not be deadly, and can even be fun.

3. Accuracy is vital for comprehension, the aim of real reading. The fourth grade boy who had no skills for unlocking big, unfamiliar words misread the word "vaccination" as "vacation." Reading gave him a different shot in the arm from the one he was expecting.

Kids whose instruction overlooks the analytical steps have no mechanism for breaking down and decoding new words: Around fourth or fifth grade, they outrun their supply of instant-recognition words and are left to either skip or guess without check-up. Either one isolates them in hit-or-miss, cut off from access to the bull's eye. These students lose the enthusiasm for reading whole language was designed to instill.

On Texture

1. Language does not develop texture spontaneously. Exposure, word play, and direct instruction are all necessary for growth.

2. Students in grades k-4 don't get language from reading, they get reading by already having language. Their language grows powerfully through what they hear read aloud.

3. Without existing vocabulary inside the student, decoding is meaningless, in the deepest sense of the word. A second grader, trying to read a simple story about the coast of Maine, struggled over the words "damp" and "mist." The teacher helped her with the blends in the first word and then asked "Do you know what damp means?" The child looked puzzled and said hesitantly, "Like garbage?" (She was thinking of dump.) The teacher helped her unlock mist, and again inquired about the meaning. The child smiled triumphantly and said "Like, you know, the school bus, and my Mom gets mad." Without the texture of descriptive vocabulary, this dogged decoder will think the coast of Maine is made of garbage and missed school busses.

When students are offered the texture but not the structure, and told they are learning to read, they want to believe it. They watch, listen, mimic, and recite. Fortunate ones take off from there. But others don't, with the resulting problem that they don't know what it is they are learning or have learned. This breeds mistrust of themselves and of their teachers. They secretly doubt that the "Magic Moment" when it all comes together will ever happen to them. The February first grader who can recite a story refrain along with the class but can't decipher the cereal box comes to mistrust his own competence in a field grown-ups take very seriously. The resultant self-doubt often breeds resistance to learning and diminished self-concept.

Why is this book about grades k-4? Carefully sequenced structural development — coupled with intellectually, emotionally, and linguistically satisfying offerings of texture running from k-4 — will launch most students on a joyful reading path. Teachers at the early end profit from knowing where their students are headed. Those in the middle years need to evaluate what is already in place and what needs teaching or reteaching. Those at the older end can readily see what holes need to be plugged and how to consolidate.

The book contains this Foreword followed by five chapters — one apiece for grades k-4. Each chapter will discuss texture — genres and facets of language children in that grade level generally enjoy. Then follows a section on structure — nuts and bolts generally appropriate for children in that grade level. Each chapter concludes with five Principles of Good Practice — specific suggestions to use right away. These are intended to be suggestive rather than comprehensive. The book concludes with an Afterword and a brief, annotated resource list.

Experience shows that the texture of whole language and the structure of phonics can form a bridge instead of a breach. Let's proceed to common ground.

Kindergarten

Texture

The way most kindergartners use language is a signpost to the type of literature, story, and word play they will enjoy. In planning the texture of what we offer, here are six points to consider.

1. Little children use language to order the universe as they see it. Labels are a powerful tool. Once you know what something is called, you can ask for it, reject it, remember it, or talk about it without its having to be physically present. This is power! The kindergarten child enjoys collecting juicy, new labels. Each one expands the child's personal catalogue of experience and emotion, and most children this age reach out eagerly for new additions. Therefore, naming books, such as those by Richard Scarry, are entertaining, instructive, and match a developmental need.

2. The kindergarten child is probably newly managing to control behavior through language. Before this, language and actions may move in opposite directions. I remember Selma Fraiberg's anecdote of the small child sitting on the kitchen floor, a box of a dozen eggs between her legs. From her mouth were coming the words "No! No! No!" But as she spoke, her hand reached for one egg after another to smash it on the floor in a glorious puddle of glop. By kindergarten, however, most children can use language to direct their impulses. For this reason, they

delight in hearing stories about ill-behaved children or impetuous creatures. *Curious George* is a nearly universal hit.

   3. Through language, the kindergarten child learns to stabilize the universe. This comes from establishing, once and for all time, the boundary line between reality and fantasy. This boundary line, in turn, allows the child to separate the logical from the ludicrous, which opens up a whole new territory of literary humor. With solid grounding in the difference between reality and fantasy, they can laugh at slapstick, which might well have been frightening instead of amusing before. One child psychologist used the example of the chef who falls down the stairs on *Sesame Street*. The child whose reality/fantasy boundary is hazy may think, "Grown-ups fall down. Grown-ups go out of control. The people who take care of me may go out of control, therefore I am not safe." Once the reality/fantasy boundary is set, the child viewer knows that Daddy and Mommy don't go rolling down huge flights of stairs, carrying platters of cream puffs. The spectacle becomes amusing. In literature, we find a match between this skill and *Sylvester and the Magic Pebble*, *Dr. DeSoto*, the poetry of Edward Lear, and some (NOT ALL) of Shel Silverstein.

   4. Kindergarten children understand and use verb tenses to arrange their thoughts, memories, and plans in sequence. This simple sounding ability represents an enormously complex abstract concept. Once the concept of time

is in place, the child can use it for governing personal behavior, particularly in learning to postpone gratification. We know from readings and personal observation that this is a cornerstone of intellectual and social growth. Because this is also a newly acquired skill, most kindergartners enjoy hearing it played out in stories with a simple sequence. They like to spot the beginning, the middle, and the end. The list of titles could stretch across the country, but one of my favorite authors is Russell Hoban. The *Frances* books are to a kindergartner what *Horatio Hornblower* or *Gone With the Wind* and its sequel are to chapter-book mavens.

5. Kindergartners are still tuning their ears to the patterns of language — learning new ones, refining old familiars, and inventing their own. For this reason, they enjoy stories with nonsense words, repetitions and refrains. Try Gloria Whelan's *A Week of Raccoons*. Research on the relationship between early language development and later reading skill shows that early enjoyment of word play and games has a high positive correlation with later powerful reading.

6. Children this age are moving from learning to love to loving to learn. For this reason they particularly enjoy interactive stories, in which the teacher reads some, and the children chime in at preordained moments. Big Books offer such experiences. So does singing. *Katy and the Big Snow* fills the bill.

Structure

Without chaining small children to chairs and force-feeding them stacks of worksheets, there are many joyful, active ways to teach some fundamentals of language structure at this level. Here are six structural elements appropriate for this level. How-to suggestions appear in the next section of this chapter, Principles of Good Practice.

1. This is the time to solidify awareness of the "wordness" of a word. Kindergartners need to learn to separate the words in a sentence, and to count how many there are. Why? Learning to hear the separate words within the stream of speech is preparation for separating words in sentences the child wants to write — keeping them apart from one another and yet connected in sense. This also paves the way for reading words on a page — making the connection between one collection of print and one spoken word. Many children need to be taught and shown that words, spoken and written, have boundaries.

2. This is the appropriate time to introduce both segmentation and blending; breaking a spoken word apart into its components (example: picnic, pic-nic), or giving a string of three, four, or five sounds, and asking the child to blend them together (example: h-a-t, b-e-s-t, s-t-a-n-d). As we will see in the next section, this can be done with a light touch — calling the roll is an ideal vehicle — or in lesson or game format. Again, research on the relationship between blending and segmentation ability and later spelling, read-

ing and writing underscores the value of showing kids how.

3. Kindergarten children, by and large, are ready to learn sound/symbol correspondence. We can make this a painless and joyfully solid opportunity by helping the children soak each letter in connotation, and then giving them a chance to use and play with what they are learning.

4. Children this age are interested in counting, and in learning how to keep track of what they have counted. For this reason, this is the correct time to teach them numerals, using multi-sensory techniques and giving them opportunities to draw their arithmetic pictorially, as well as record it in the symbolic notation of numerals.

5. Many children can learn to recognize their own names, and perhaps some of their friends', at this age. Adults should provide the opportunity. Some children who are slated to be sight readers will show easy word recognition at this level. We should encourage them to exercise this skill, meanwhile downplaying its importance for the long run, and reminding parents that reading and academic success are not determined by who is first off the starting block.

6. A large percentage of kindergartners won't deduce or induce sound/symbol correspondence from looking at books being read to them. Within this percentage, probably 15-20% have the patterns associated with Learn-

ing Disabilities, Specific Language Disability, or the Dyslexias. They will need multi-sensory teaching to analyze what print offers and to be able to produce written language themselves. There is no short cut here.

Five Principles of Good Practice

1. Teach "The Letter of the Week." Personally, I have seen the greatest success in classrooms using the sequence laid out by Nina Traub in *Recipe for Reading*. Each letter builds on the one before it, and confusing look-alikes are well separated.

Write the letter on the board, demonstrate its correct formation, give the sound, and a few words which begin with the sound. Ask the children if they can think of others for the collection.

As much as possible, dovetail art projects. (I saw one class making velvet valentines for *v* week.)

2. Sound/Symbol Cards. Because connotation helps children remember the arbitrarily designed, two-dimensional symbols we call letters, we do well to capitalize on the success of this strategy. As a class together and as individuals, the children make clue cards, which, when collected together on a ring, make an excellent tool for teaching, review, and games. The trick here is to have the clue material start with the sound the letter makes. For example, following Nina Traub's sequence, the clue for *c* is

cotton balls. The children glue little cotton balls in the shape of a *c* on the *c* card. For the *a* card, they superimpose a drawing (their own) of an apple on top of the letter *a*, then color it. The *d* on the *d* card is made by round, stick-on label dots. The *g* on the *g* card is made from a cut-up pair of party-favor sunglasses (green if possible), arranged with the eye piece forming the round part of the letter and the ear piece hanging down as the hook.

Once each child has ten or more letter cards on a notebook ring, the way is open for all sorts of games. ("I'm going to make a sound. You turn to the card that makes my sound.") The fact that they have pasted on those *c*otton balls or *d*ots or *y*ellow *y*arn themselves, while making and rehearsing the sound, is a pride-inducing memory aid. Little kids, like the rest of us, enjoy doing what they do well. With a ring of letter cards, practice is fun.

The letter of the week can extend into whatever literature is planned for that time: "Can we think of any *g* words to describe Curious George?"

Although *Recipe for Reading* was originally developed for use with dyslexic students, schools which use its multi-sensory methods and carefully developed sequence for all students find a rise in reading competence and pleasure, a drop in referrals to the Resource Room or outside tutoring, and an increased sense of autonomy and competence among the teachers. Pretty hard to beat!

For those who are interested, here is a list of clue materials developed by teachers at our school:

a: apple superimposed on the letter *a*

b: balloon pasted on card in shape of a *b*

c: cotton balls in shape of a *c*

d: dots pasted in shape of a *d*

e: beaten egg used to trace/paint *e*

f: feathers pasted in shape of an *f*

g: green (toy) sunglasses cut & pasted in shape of a *g*

h: red hearts drawn or punched out and pasted in shape of an *h*

i: an Indian drawn straight and tall like an *i*

j: jam or jelly used to "paint" the *j*

k: crinkled foil wrapping from Hershey's Kisses pasted in shape of a *k*

l: lollipop sticks pasted in shape of an *l*

m: mini-marshmallows pasted in shape of an *m*

n: nails used to form *n*

o: tongue depressor decorated with *o*'s

p: paper cut out to form *p*

q: quilt drawn as the background on the card

r: raisins arranged in shape of an *r*

s: string arranged in shape of an *s*

t: colored tape used to form a *t*

u: ugly face drawn inside the letter *u*

v: velvet arranged in shape of a *v*

w: letter is drawn in open part of a wig

x: x-ray drawn on card
y: yellow yarn arranged in shape of a *y*
z: paper letter decorated with zebra stripes pasted on card

3. Each child makes a sound/symbol scrapbook, one page per letter in the beginning. Add more pages per letter as the occasion demands. Pictures may be cut out from magazines or catalogues, or drawn by the children themselves.

4. Keeping a calendar. Time is an invisible concept. It is only accessible through language and through visual aids. Since understanding time is such a vital part of reading comprehension, this is a good time to play with sequence and such terms as "today," "tomorrow," "three days ago," trying to avoid the confusion behind Michael's word "nexterday". If the teacher writes one "letter-of-the-week word" on the calendar describing something about that day, and then even draws a little accompanying rebus, the group has material for discussion: "Remember three days ago...that was the day we said was *b*lustery and we had to cover up well. The day after that, two days ago, was *b*etter, and yesterday was *b*eautiful!" As the teacher moves her hand back and forth across the days being remembered or anticipated, the children connect their own experiences and words with the sweep of time, and its notation on the calendar. This lays the groundwork for later understanding "flashbacks," "fast forward," or simply "first," "next," "then," "finally."

5. Word play for kindergartners should include games of rhyming, alliteration, segmentation, and blending.

Rhyming comes easily to some children, with difficulty to others, and some don't really catch on until they see the words written down. Start by offering a stimulus and two choices, one of which makes a rhyme. (cat: sun or fat? Try to avoid mixing association and rhyming, as in cat: whiskers or fat?) Then toss out a word and ask the child to make his own rhyme (nonsense words are entirely permissible). Call the roll by saying the child's name, then giving a word. Instead of answering "here," the child should reply by giving a rhyming word.

Alliteration games work well in a circle. Give one child a word to start with, then each child around the circle must continue by giving a word beginning with the same sound. I heard one kindergarten class come up with over one hundred *l* words in one five-minute sitting. The words ranged from "little" to "lollipop" to "lollapaloozer" to "lemonade" to "leviathan!"

Segmentation is a vital and undertaught skill which lends itself beautifully to what the children think of as games. See the Resources Section for information about Jerome Rosner's book, *Helping Children Overcome Learning Difficulties*. He designed the series of exercises which move from "say picnic...say it again without the *nic*" to "say smack...say it again without the *m*." We don't need to stay up all night writing segmentation problems. Rosner has done it for us, beautifully sequenced, showing exactly where to start.

Blending is a major pre-reading skill easy to practice in a lighthearted way. Again, try using roll call. "I'll call your name and say some sounds or syllables; see if you can squish them together to make a familiar word." Just look around the room for plenty of ideas: sweat-er, c-u-p, par-ka, etc.

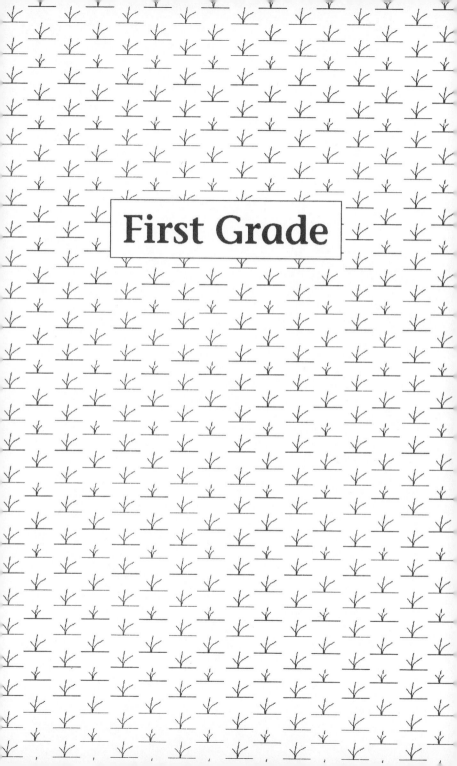

First Grade

First grade is generally the child's introduction to formal instruction in language arts: reading, writing, and spelling. Before moving to the twin topics of texture and structure, let's review some thoughts on reading.

Because most people read sitting down, some think of it as passive. Yet true reading, like true learning, is aggressively active. The word "comprehension," in fact, comes from the Latin word "prehendere," meaning to seize.

Reading is an interactive process through which the reader connects print on the page with his or her own experience and emotions, supply of general knowledge, and existing vocabulary. In addition to harnessing intellectual, psychological and linguistic energies, readers use their eyes, their ears, and their muscles.

Reading has lasting effects when it follows a three-step progression: take in, think over, and put out. The middle step is often overlooked in school, however, in the press to "finish a unit," or "cover the material." I prefer the truism "The purpose of education is not to cover a subject, but to uncover it."

Texture

Here are five comments about first graders, their use of language, and how this use influences their literary tastes.

1. One of the central psychological jobs of early childhood is to develop a sense of what makes the world tick. Little children use their eyes and ears as they try to figure out what makes things happen and why the world works the way it does. Language is the tool which helps them go beyond what they can see and hear directly, and lays bare for them some of the gears and machinery of everyday phenomena.

Most first graders have established a sense of cause and effect. This beckons them into stories requiring them to use logic. Stories which require anticipation and prediction as well as logic tickle their fancies. Most first graders also have the intellectual stamina to carry details over from one chapter to another. For these reasons, *My Father's Dragon*, and its two sequels, meet first graders where they are, and ignite their imaginations as well as their intellects.

2. Because most first graders have established the boundary between reality and fantasy we discussed in the previous chapter, they like to prove their new power to themselves. With the superiority of converts, they like to flirt with what had previously been confusing issues. They welcome the shiver of recognition that comes with listening to a story in which animal characters or children shift back and forth between the two kingdoms. For this reason, they enjoy stories about giants, about talking cats, about pinch-faced aunts and flying peaches, about trains that talk, or about badgers who give advice.

3. Inside most first graders is a ferocious wrestling match. Fair and unfair slug it out daily, and generally, by the middle of the school year, fair is firmly established. This is not to say all first grade behavior is governed by rules of equity, but most of the children understand, inside themselves and among one another, what constitutes fair.

For this reason, they enjoy fairy tales in which justice always wins out. Some adults fear that since each fairy tale concludes with a revenge finale, children will be unduly frightened or led morally astray. Should the endings be softened, or Bowdlerized? We are wise to remember the comments of G.K. Chesterton, who said that adults, being corrupt, prefer mercy; children, being innocent, prefer justice.

Fairy tales come in many versions, illustrated by a wide variety of artists. It is possible to find versions compatible with the adult's point of view. Myself, I remember the gleam of satisfaction in generations of children's eyes when they hear that the wicked queen was forced to dance to death in red-hot iron shoes.

Most first graders, being small, enjoy stories in which the little triumphs over the big. For this reason, folk tales and some kinds of ethnic lore are meat and drink. Classic patterns here include the victory of the scorned youngest child (Cinderella, Cinderlad to name but two), the might of the seemingly weak (David and Goliath), the small animal with great power (*The Lion and the Mouse*, or

Puss in Boots), or the magic in a common-looking object or incantation (*Aladdin and the Magic Lamp*, and any magic wand stories).

4. Along these same lines, first graders enjoy seeing themselves as major contributors to the general good of the world. They will talk enthusiastically about the missions they will accomplish when they grow up. For this reason a book such as *Miss Rumphius* legitimizes their sense of important work to be done in life, now as well as later.

5. Finally, although this would not satisfy adult literary tastes, in fairness to children we must remember that they enjoy the very act of decoding for itself. They are like little 007's getting in on a secret, prying open what had previously been closed to them.

Richard Masland, M.D., makes the point that early reading — first grade and part of second — is primarily a form of pattern recognition. Later, in third grade the reader switches over to linguistic recognition. These two activities occur in different parts of the brain, and the accomplished adult reader needs to have laid both foundations.

So, while sophisticated adults may not want to spend a winter evening curled up by the fire with a copy of *Mac and Tab*, we mustn't deny the pleasure to little children who find it deeply satisfying.

Structure

First graders are ready to learn the sounds and letter formation of the following structural elements:

Consonants

Vowels

Digraphs (ch, th, sh, wh)

Ing, ang, ong, ung, ink, ank, unk

"Magic e" (in which the e added at the end of the word makes the vowel long)

Consonant blends in initial and final positions, starting with two letters and expanding to three (stop, band, stand, strand, skirts)

The words for colors and numbers

The 5 wh words: who, what, when, where, why

They also need to continue practicing how to break words apart into segments, and how to blend sounds or sound clusters into whole words.

Why are the above important? Let four first graders' words speak.

On mastering phonics. "I like it when I know how to do stuff. It makes me feel safe."

On the reliability of letters to make words. A first grader couldn't locate her reading book. Her teacher said,

"Here. Try this book instead," holding out a book at the same reading level which contained much of the same vocabulary as her customary book. "No," said the child fearfully. "I don't know how to read that book." "I'll help you," said the teacher. "You know almost all the words on this first page." "Wait!" said the child, astonishment spreading over her face, "You mean they use the same words in different books!"

On giving courage. "I can't read this. The words are too fat." "Here. I'll show you what to do. Cover up the *s* at the end and see what's left." "B-a-n-d ... band. Oh, I get it, bands."

On putting knowledge to work. A first grader who had changed schools in the middle of the year went from a phonics/linguistics program into a look/say, whole word recognition classroom. Her second day, she threw her book on the floor, saying with disgust "This dumb book doesn't read!"

My mother was a New Englander who raised me with a proverb for almost every occasion. One of her favorites was "Fine words butter no parsnips." We are ready for the practical suggestions in Principles of Good Practice.

Five Principles of Good Practice

1. Daily dictation gives the children a chance to use the sounds they have been hearing and seeing. Putting words on paper reinforces sound/symbol correspondence and opens the way to increasing prowess in creative writing. In the most successful models I have seen, the teacher structures a lesson around the sound or sounds they are working on that day. First showing and sounding, then sounding and making the letter on the board, the teacher demonstrates. Then she asks the students to make the letters in the air, or on their desk tops with their fingers, and finally distributes the paper. She dictates a series of sounds or words, then a phrase, then a sentence using the sound, and then gives the children a chance to illustrate what they have written.

A lesson on the /a/ sound (as in cat) might have as dictation "/a/; please make five of that letter. Circle the one you think is your very best. I'll give you three words, one at a time. Listen, repeat, and write: mad, sat, nap. Good. Now here's a phrase: a sad cat. Please write it and then draw me the saddest cat you can make. We'll take time to look at one another's pictures."

A variation involves dictating an incomplete sentence and asking the children to finish it in their own way: "Dan had..." Obviously, the children's responses aren't limited to /a/ words. Using invented spelling, they can say anything they want. They are liberated from only being able to write words they have "had."

Children genuinely enjoy feeling their competence mount, and dictation given with an eye to opportunities for originality is not repressive but expressive.

A nice wrap-up or review is to have five containers, one per vowel. I use a basket, pot, pitcher, mug, and egg (plastic from L'Eggs pantyhose). In the basket I put a set of cards each with an /a/ word, a set of /o/ words in the pot, /i/ words in the pitcher, /u/ words in the mug, and /e/ words in the egg. I ask each child to come and take one card from each container, reading the words to me, one container at a time. If a child misses, all I have to say is "Basket words say /a/."

Recipe for Reading contains word lists. Teachers have enough to do without having to reinvent the wheel.

2. Vowel and Digraph Rings. Vowel sounds are hard to discriminate from one another, and hard for some children to remember. When they jog their own memories through their personal art work, the task gets easier. Here's how. Give each child a notebook ring and five index cards. In the lower right hand corner of each index card, write one of the vowels. Give each student one card. Say "Here's the letter *a*. It says /a/. Can you think of some words that have /a/ in the middle? Good. Now choose one of those words, and draw a picture of that word on your *a* card." The

budding Leonardo who draws an alligator or an arrow, or even the old favorite apple, will remember the sound and associate it with the letter.

Go through the five vowels that way. When all students have five illustrated cards on their rings, they each have an invaluable self-help tool, and game material. ("I'm going to say a word. Turn to the vowel card of the sound you hear in the middle of my word.")

Use the same strategy to teach and reinforce digraph sounds. One first grade artist drew an elephant on an escalator for his *e* card, and a ship and a sheep in a shop for his *sh* digraph. Repression of creativity? Hardly. Using imagination and personal connotation to teach arbitrary symbols? Yes.

3. Mix and Match Games. Make a chart listing color words in the left-hand column and corresponding blocks of color on the right-hand column. This is the self-help material. Then take an even number of index cards. On one card write the color word, on the other card put a line or block in the color. Shuffle the cards. Give them to the child to sort and match. Leave the self-help poster in clear view. Provide a few hints as the child gets going. "Let's see, your color is green. What letter would green start with? End with? Good, now you can use process of elimination as you sort through the words."

Use the same strategy for teaching the number words — match the numeral with a pictorial representation. Try to use the same configurations one finds on dice. Be sure to leave the self-help strategy chart in plain view.

A similar strategy works for teaching discrimination of the *wh* words: who, what, when, where, why. These start-alikes are confusing to many early readers. But children catch on quickly when they realize that who asks a question about people, when about time, where about place, what about a thing, and why about a reason. On the self-help chart, list the words on the left and the words with a rebus inserted on the right.

who	**wh☺**
what	**wh🎁t**
when	**wh⊜n**
where	**wher➤e**
why	**why?**

Bingo works well for teaching sight words. Make a 9" square grid on a plain piece of paper. Photocopy or run it on the ditto so you have a good supply. Write out nine words you want to teach. Write nine corresponding cards. Ask the child first to simply match the word on the card to the word in the space. Next, call out the word and see if the child can select it. Finally, give the child the word cards, asking him or her to read the word and put it on its matching space. The progression of match, select, and read works well and eliminates fear.

4. *Zoo.* Tell the children they are going to invent some new species of animals. Find a tray with seven compartments, or use seven small paper bags. In each compartment or bag, put words and letters in the following categories:

> *numbers*
> *colors*
> *adjectives*
> *body parts*
> *initial consonants or consonant blends*
> *vowels*
> *final consonants or consonant blends*

Give each child a piece of paper with the heading "A New Animal" and the opening sentence "My new animal has ____ ____ ____ ____ and is called a ____." Each child picks one card from each compartment or bag in order, and ends up with something such as "My new animal has six yellow wooly ears and is called a Stug."

Ask the children to draw their animals, show them to their classmates, introduce the animals to one another. Which ones do they think will be natural friends, and why? Which ones will fight, and how? The possibilities spin on everlastingly. What kind of habitat would your animal have, what kinds of food does it need, is it an animal to tame or one which needs to be wild, is it related to any existing species, what makes you think so? In art class, or as a home or classroom project, the children can make puppets of their animals. They can turn the classroom into a zoo and invite other groups to come for a visit.

This exercise in reading and using words, and in blending letters into nonsensical but pronounceable words, is a perfect way to practice phonics while putting the imagination on a trampoline. It is simplicity itself to join the newly created animals to the ongoing reading.

5. Interactive Stories. Here is a way to combine reading practice, suspense, creative writing, and humor with the first graders' linguistic developmental level. From *Recipe for Reading* (or another word list source of your choice), select ten or twenty words in the sound pattern the class is studying. Weave those words into a story.

In my case, I use a porcelain doll named Miss Peaches. She sits in a small rocking chair in the classroom and all the children know her. I hold her up and say "You probably think that Miss Peaches stays in school all week-end while you are home or outside playing. Well, let me tell you a secret. When I came into school today, I found this note on my desk. I'm going to copy it on the board, you read it as I write, and we'll see what it says."

As I write, the children read aloud. They are decoding, anticipating, checking up on their guesses and hunches, and hearing a story all at the same time. Then I leave them, *Perils of Pauline* style, in the middle of a terrible dilemma and ask them to write the rest of the story, telling how the heroine will escape. We read the children's ideas together, and I pick up the narrative, taking it one step farther the next day, all the while incorporating letter and sound combinations from the cluster we are studying.

Here's a sample from February.

"Dear Mrs. Vail,

A magic bubble came down onto my lap and whispered, 'Let's go on a surprise trip.' I said, 'O.K.' We blew in the darkness to the far side of the moon, where we came to a very big castle. When we went in, we saw good things to eat: cake with frosting, little colored candies, and fancy sandwiches. We heard music. A frog was playing the flute and a kangaroo played the fiddle. A voice said 'Enjoy yourself, my dear.' In came a very ugly witch with warts on her nose and long filthy hair. I felt scared. The magic bubble told me we should leave. Just as I floated out the window to safety, I heard another voice say, 'Please come back and rescue me. I am a princess. The witch has put me in a small dark room. I am guarded by a troll with two heads.'"

"Children, please find a way to help the princess escape."

The children wrote their ideas, and the next day the story continued:

"When the repulsive two-headed troll saw that the princess had escaped, he stamped his feet in rage. He stamped and stomped and whomped so hard that one of his toenails fell off. He yelled and hollered and blustered and shouted, 'Revenge! Death to the princess. I will teach her not to play tricks on me!'

The princess was inside the magic bubble with Miss Peaches and they floated, in silence, near enough to hear the ugly troll's wild words. 'Oh, no,' sobbed the princess in fear. 'Now both the witch of the castle and the troll of the prison want to punish me. And here is a terrible truth. I was in such a hurry to escape that I left behind my rag doll, who is not a doll at all, but is really my small sister, put under a spell by the witch. If I return, the troll and the witch will kill me. But I cannot abandon my sister. What can I do?'"

Had these passages been presented to the children in print, densely spaced as they are here, some students would have felt overwhelmed. But if they are reading aloud as I write on the board, I can pace the words to their facility.

Efficient teaching for joyful learning incorporates clear explanations, joining as many senses as possible, offering immediate chances to practice newly learned skills, and showcasing imagination and prowess. As frequently as possible, I ask the children to illustrate what they have written or heard. In forming and crystallizing their own imagery to accompany what they hear, they are exercising the mind's eye, a premium path to strong reading comprehension.

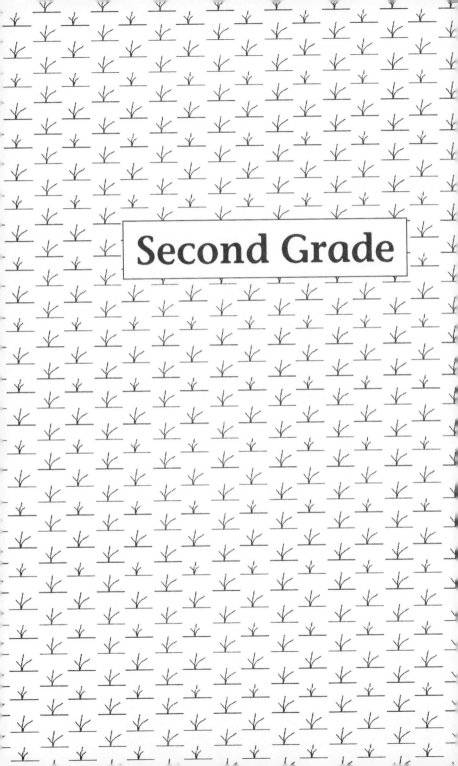

Second Grade

Second graders are apt to be more mercurial than first graders. Their parents may ask, "Where is the sunny child from last year?" To the children's own surprise (and the dismay of their parents), they still cry in public and often are moody and vulnerable. Because they are uncertain, they don't like to be taken by surprise. Internal disequilibrium, a symptom of growth, points most children this age to-wards enjoyment of particular types and genres of reading and listening. This in turn governs their enthusiasms for what they write.

Texture

Here are five comments about developmental levels and related literary tastes.

1. Most second graders are eager to accumulate factual information about people, history, geography, and the sociology of other cultures. Waist-high anthropolo-gists, they delve into the ways of the Navajo, the artifacts of Asia, or problems besetting farmers. Given a chance to make tabletop models, a group of second graders armed with clay, toothpicks, string, paint, a few feathers, and bits of art trouve demonstrate their knowledge with flair and enthusiasm.

Because their sense of their own regional culture has moved from fluid to stable, they are able to appreciate other places and other times. This points to literature about children in other places and times, and to hearing factual descriptions from junior resource books.

To help in the expansion of knowledge, try *The Magic Schoolbus* series.

2. Second graders wavering between feelings of power and vulnerability often gravitate toward tales of protection and rescue. These give the child the opportunity to identify with both the rescuer and the rescuee. *Mio, My Son* by Astrid Lindgren and *Matilda* by Roald Dahl are two to read aloud.

Probably their powerful fear of being on their own without adult protection accounts for the popularity of stories about children who manage without grown-ups. In the movies, we have had the phenomenal box-office success of *Home Alone*, and generations of children have cut their eyeteeth of solitary courage on *Pippi Longstocking*.

3. Second graders have usually accumulated the nuts and bolts of everyday working vocabulary. They can ask for specific items by name. ("Please hand me the *hammer*," or the *wrench*, or the *screwdriver*, perhaps even the *Phillips Head screwdriver*, instead of the *thingy* or *it*.) They are ready to add on the vocabulary of ornamentation. They have an exquisite appetite for beautiful words, coursing cadences, or the surf sounds of rhythm, lap, and crash in prose or poetry. Old-fashioned verse seems to appeal. Such A.A. Milne favorites as Bold Sir Brian Botany who "walked

among the villagers and blipped them on the head" bring smiles and heads nodding in time with the verse. Hilaire Belloc's *Cautionary Verses*, Edward Lear's limericks, or Provenson's *Our Animal Friends at Maple Hill Farm* are a few samples.

4. Because most second graders' sense of cause and effect is stable, they enjoy fooling around with the instability of sound-alike words, and the jokes or stories born of misperception. *Amelia Bedelia* sends them rolling in the aisles. And many of them are good enough readers to turn the myriad of joke books for this age into family torture hour.

5. Second graders enjoy playing with nonsense words. We must remember that simply because word play is vital nourishment for kindergartners and first graders, it isn't too babyish for second graders. They need to continue with rhyming, alliteration, segmentation, and blending. Now they are also ready for onomatopoeia, in which a word makes the very same sound it describes: the buzzing of the bees, the rumbling of the thunder. What, pray, is a "runcible spoon?" Second graders can even learn that big word if we break it down for them: on-a-mat-o-pea-ya. Doubtful? Which grade in school gets the biggest charge out of "supercalafragilisticexpealidocious?"

Structure

Following are seven structural elements suitable for second graders. By laying the foundations when the children are ready, instead of waiting with free-floating optimism for them to catch on independently, we do them the service of providing a platform for later growth, as well as satisfaction at the moment.

1. Vowel teams and diphthongs (*ai, ay, ea, ou, ow, au, aw, oi, oy*, etc.)

2. *ild, old, ost* words (child, cold, most)

3. Awareness of endings as units: *s, ing, ed* (3 pronunciations: /ed/, /d/, and /t/ as in landed, named, or jumped)

4. Consolidation of sound/symbol correspondence to an automatic level

5. Development of ease in handwriting. First and second graders care passionately about the appearance of their work, and we are wise to capitalize on this enthusiasm. The development of what the neurologists call "kinetic melody" is a major source of strength as the student progresses through school. The child who does not consolidate this skill is headed for school problems starting in fourth or fifth grades. Second grade is the time to notice who has achieved lift-off and who needs extra training.

Those who need a boost should get it now, when they are still interested in the task.

6. Sight vocabulary for reading should include the roughly 225 words of highest frequency. Lists of these can be found in almost any manual on the teaching of reading.

7. Syllable counting, and awareness of a syllable as a segment of a word.

Five Principles of Good Practice

1. Daily dictation, begun in first grade, should continue. The principles remain the same, although the format should expand to match the children's growing competence. The material dictated and written should include the sound combinations under study, and also incorporate some extraneous material. For example, one teacher says, "Today's dictation will have five sentences. I'll give them to you one at a time. Please listen, repeat, and write. Our letter and sound pattern is *ai*, so lots of the words will contain *ai*. Now here's something else. When you have all five sentences, you will have the description of someone in the room. DON'T TELL WHO IT IS, but draw a picture of something that person has on. Ready? Here we go. 'X is not in jail. X lives on Main St. In summer, X likes to sail and keep hermit crabs in a pail. X has a brown pony tail.'"

2. File-Folder Games. Take a stack of manila file folders and give each a cover title incorporating one or two

of the vowel teams to be learned. Open the folder and draw a game board path. Mark the path off into units, and in each one write a word. Save three or four units for surprise messages. Give each player a token, use one die, advance along the path according to the number on the die, reading each word you land on. If a child stumbles on a word, say, "Remember the name of the game. The name has the sound in it: Owl's House. *Ou* says /ow/, *ow* says /ow/."

The game path might look like this:

See *Recipe for Reading* for word lists. A surprise space might be "You shouted in the house. Lose 1 turn." Or, "You can be proud, go ahead 3 spaces." Four or five surprise spaces keep second graders in high anticipation. A box of small toys to use as tokens increases the fun.

Here are some suggested game titles:

Owl's House
The Mean Beast Feasts
Daily Mail
Pay Day
Stay in Jail
Read for Real
Healthy Bread

Let the children make an illustration to go on the cover. Ten or fifteen file-folder games will bring a lot of laughs and teach a lot of sounds.

3. Read and Draw. Write a set of drawing directions on the board, incorporating the sounds and sight words you want the children to practice. Color code the punctuation so the periods are bright red. Say, "Take out a piece of paper. Read the whole set of instructions to yourself. Then read the sentences one at a time, and draw what it tells you to. The periods are red to remind you where the sentences stop. At the end, we will share our pictures. Here's something interesting. Even though twenty children will be reading the same directions, and using the same size paper, all the pictures will be different. It will be fun to see how they are the same and how they are different."

Here's a sample:

Draw a hill. On the hill draw six pine trees. In the

sky draw two clouds. On one of the clouds, draw a bird. At the bottom of the hill, draw a pond. In the pond put three different kinds of fish. Draw a boy fishing. Put a red hat on him. Draw a dog near the trees. In the bottom right-hand corner, draw a pile of stones. Somewhere in the picture put something you would like to get for your birthday.

4. Builders and Dismantlers — games for two-syllable words.

Pic-nic. Take a stack of index cards. With scissors, dog-ear the upper left hand corner of the cards. On each card write a two-syllable word broken apart in the middle. Make a master list of the words. Then cut the cards in half. Shuffle the pieces. Spread them around on the floor or a table. Can the child(ren) put the pieces together to restore the words? (The reason for dog-earing is so everyone knows right away which piece is the first half and which the last half.)

Moon Food. Start with the same materials and preparation. Then give each child a piece of paper with the heading "Moon Food." A first sentence reads "Welcome to the Moon's finest restaurant. Today we will be serving:" The rest of the paper is laid out like a menu with blanks to be filled in. The children choose two cards, put them together to make a nonsense word, pronounce it, decide whether it sounds like a soup, main course, dessert, beverage or salad, and then write the names in the blanks. Children swap menus and see if they can read each others'.

5. Word Trains and Compound Words.

Word trains are built by starting with an engine word, and then adding word cars which start with the ending letter of the word ahead. (Example: Engine word is "hamburger," followed by rain, net, tent, try, yellow, win, never, etc.)

Compound words are made of two words which stand on their own alone. For example, handbag is made of hand and bag. Each is a word. Over time, collect compound words from the group. Make a train of them and see how many times you can keep it growing along the walls of the classroom. Hint: "classroom" qualifies.

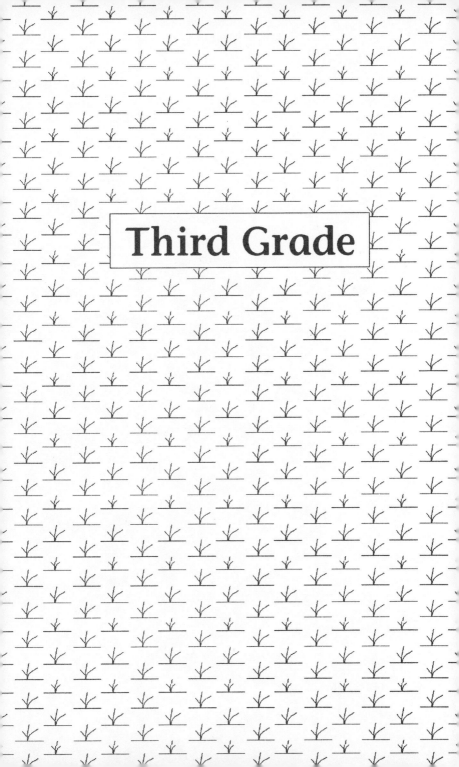

Third Grade

In third grade, reading shifts from being the goal of the curriculum to becoming a tool for academic exploration. We remember from Dr. Masland's comments, cited in the chapter on first grade, that around third grade reading switches over from pattern recognition to linguistic recognition. But the word "recognition" implies pre-existing knowledge; you don't recognize something never seen before. Linguistic recognition flows from an existing pool of language within the child. This includes, but also goes beyond, straight vocabulary, encompassing recognition of constructions, rhythms, and cadence. Familiarity with these gives the reader the ability to anticipate what the writer is about to say. This is called either "anticipatory schemata," or more graphically, "casting a linguistic shadow." Active reading, in which the reader recognizes and anticipates, is a joyful, active pursuit which develops in most children at third grade.

Thus, third graders need a rich supply of internal language to enjoy their own capacities. As adults, we must be sure that the textural and structural aspects of language laid out for younger children are firmly in place by third grade. If they are not, now is the time to plug the holes and make up for deficits.

Texture

Here are five aspects of linguistic texture which match third graders' appetites.

1. Third graders enjoy their newly developing skills of verbal negotiation. Playground disputes, classroom arguments, and consideration of intellectual or social issues resolve through verbal reasoning, instead of physical possession or prowess.

Enter the pun, the joking insult, verbal banter and badinage, and clubs with, of course, secret passwords. At this level, the children enjoy stories of social situations, and find the language of social relationships is both interesting and entertaining. Beverly Cleary's *Ramona* is a favorite.

2. Interest in double meanings opens the way to stories and jokes built on homonyms (steal/steel) or homographs (present/present). Fred Gwynne's *The King Who Rained* is one title among many in this genre.

3. Myths and folk tales about different origins of common phenomena are intellectually and developmentally appropriate. Third graders enjoy discovering different cultures' ideas about the first rainbow, the origin of fire, the advent of the seasons. And, of course, as they read, we should encourage them to invent and write their own. Try *In the Beginning* and other Virginia Hamilton anthologies.

Moving farther into mythic territory, D'Aulaire's *Norse Gods and Giants* and *Greek Myths* are written in beautiful language, they explore fundamental questions, and the individual pieces are an appropriate length for reading aloud. Third graders, searching out questions of loyalty, power, rivalry, deceit, revenge, and affection, are keenly interested in the mythic archetypes of trickster, ruler, protector, warrior, and hero.

One example of a classic hero's journey is Maurice Sendak's *Where the Wild Things Are.* Two other titles are *Maggie B.* and *Brave Irene.* For a tale combining a journey and courage, read *The Tale of Jumping Mouse.*

4. As third graders solidify their internal language of time and space, they enjoy hearing stories rich in setting, and moving backwards and forwards through time. This happens either through flashbacks and fast forwards in narrative, or through physics, as in Madeleine L'Engle's *Wrinkle in Time.*

Third graders should have intuitive and precise understanding of the concept of time. This is the moment for a checkup. Students should know days of the week, months of the year, seasons, hours in a day, division of day into A.M. and P.M. They also need orderly organization of their own experiences into distant past, recent past, present, and future. Access to the future, which is of course invisible, depends on a sense of logical anticipation. This in turn rests on a clear understanding of what is now, and what has come before.

The ready availability of digital watches has camouflaged temporal confusion in many of today's kids. It's one thing to call out the numbers on a watch (8:42) and quite another to know that means there are 18 minutes until nine o'clock, and what the unfolding of 18 minutes feels like. Confusion over elapsing time is at the bottom of many academic problems arising in third grade. Kids don't have the sense of how long something takes to do.

5. Third graders need to hear rumbly, big stories. To fill their ears and hearts with the might of language and the power of narrative is to nourish them on a fundamental level. A tragically large number of today's children are fed on verbal fast food instead. They digest and produce what I think of as the "Golden Arches of McLanguage." We need to do everything in our power to compensate for this malnutrition. Many old favorites are available for this purpose, but for a change try William Steig's *The Bad Island*.

Structure

Expanding the foundations laid in previous years, here are three structural elements third graders need to learn.

1. With good early training, they already know how to count syllables in a word, keep them in order, or rearrange them. Now they need to learn to recognize, read, and spell the six different kinds of syllables. Because it's unfair to ask teachers to explain things they've never been taught themselves, here's a quick brush-up for those who need it.

Closed syllable: consonant-vowel-consonant (cvc) in which the vowel has the short sound. (Example: cat, bed, him, log, cut.)

Open syllable: consonant-vowel (cv) in which the vowel has the long sound. (Example: ba as in baby, he as in hero, gi as in giant, so as in solo, hu as in human.)

"Magic e," in which the e added at the end of the word makes the vowel long. (Example: lake, Pete, mile, pole, huge.)

R controlled, in which the presence of r changes the sound of the vowel. (Example: bar, her, firm, word, fur.)

Consonant-le in which the word ending is a syllable unto itself. (Example: bat-tle, waf-fle, gig-gle, ti-tle, ri-fle, etc.)

Rule benders which do not fit the 85% regular pattern of English. (Example: one, the, could.)

Those interested in further information on this, and in an extensive supply of word lists, should consult *Recipe for Reading* or any of the other materials listed in Resources.

2. Chunking. For both reading and spelling, third graders need automatic recognition of such common chunks in words as *ing, ed, ful, pre, non, un,* etc. Recognition of these

chunks as reliable and frequently occurring units helps in accurate decoding of polysyllabic words. For whatever reason, research and experience show that most errors in reading long words involve distortion or omission of the third syllable. Therefore, if we prepare our students to mentally isolate the beginning and end of a long unfamiliar word, we are reducing their likelihood of error in the middle.

3. Maintenance of vowel discrimination. A very high percentage of spelling rules require knowing the difference between the long and short sound of a vowel. Yet this discrimination, taught in the earlier years, is often overlooked when children reach third grade. Ironically, this is just when many spelling rules are formally taught, or when children are expected to know them by heart, parrot them on demand, and use them in creative endeavors. Knowing when to double the consonant (batting and biting), when to use *ge* or *dge* (huge, fudge), what to drop when adding *ing* (making, running) depends on accurate vowel discrimination. Let's, as they say, keep up the good work!

Five Principles of Good Practice

1. Daily dictation, begun in first grade, can continue right along at a more sophisticated level. One or two sentences should probe and practice syllable work, another should contain a homonym or be a pun, and the final one should be an open-ended beginning for the student to finish independently. The practice of hearing, thinking, saying, and writing is excellent training for spontaneous writing, in which the author takes dictation to his or her hand from his or her own ears and mind.

Handwriting instruction should continue. Automatic mechanical flow is the key to powerful, joyful composition. Two ten-minute exercises are better than one long session. Homework is a fine vehicle for practice.

2. Combined with, or alternating with, dictation should be proofreading practice. The teacher puts a sentence or two on the board. When the children come in in the morning, they look at it, spot the errors individually, then the group corrects it together as the teacher makes the necessary repairs on the board. Sample sentences are in *Daily Oral Language* by Neil J. Vail and Joseph F. Papenfuss.

3. *Old Made/Old Maid.* Take a stack of colored index cards (white ones are too transparent). Make a list of homonym pairs on a chart. This will be the self-help device. After each word, make a little rebus encapsulating the meaning. If there is a student artist in the group, assign the task to him or her. Then take pairs of index cards, and on each one write one word of the pair. Put in one extra card. I get my Old Maid by having one homonym trio (to, too, two). Shuffle and deal the cards, playing according to the rules of Old Maid. Players pick cards from one another in turn, making pairs when possible and putting pairs face

up on the table. The player left with the single card is the loser. In this game, I require players to use each homonym of a pair in a sentence as part of being allowed to discard.

The pairs of homonym cards can also be used for a version of Concentration.

4. Syllable Counts. Taking attendance is a fine vehicle for practicing this skill. Call each child's name, and tell him or her a word. The child is to respond with the number of syllables in the word. The teacher then asks the child to spell out either the first, second, third, fourth or fifth syllable. This is excellent preparation for attempting to spell long, important, unrehearsed or untaught words, and a light-hearted way to continue the training in segmentation begun earlier. Exercises in this skill pay enormous dividends in spelling and writing, not to mention reading.

5. The Three R's. Read, rehearse, record. Many children in today's society are already nostalgic for their own childhoods. They didn't get quite enough. Here's a way to let them go back for seconds while still moving forward. Ask each one to choose three or four favorite books from their earlier years. Let them reread to their hearts' content. Then ask them to rehearse reading the stories aloud. Finally, ask them to record the stories on a tape recorder, and take the tape to the kindergartners or first graders.

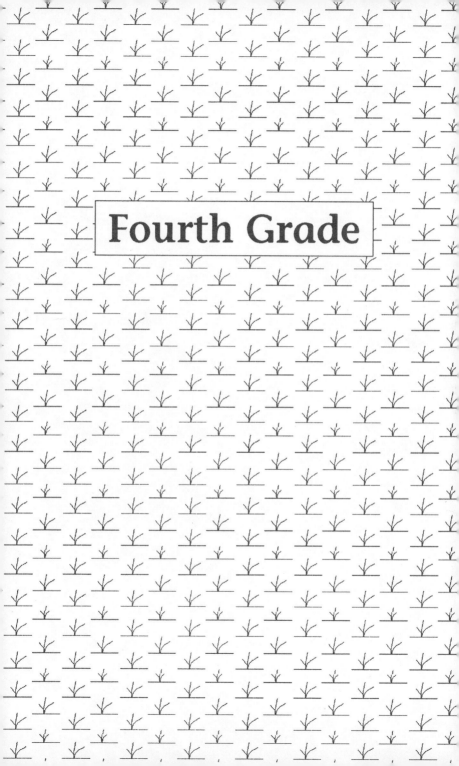

Fourth Grade

Fourth graders are changing physically, psychologically, and intellectually before our very eyes, but rates of development vary widely from one to another. As adults, we sometimes need to remind ourselves that the boy who has grown taller than his teacher is not automatically as mature as an adult. While we admire their developing muscles and varieties of prowess, we must factor fourth graders' vulnerabilities into our teaching, our offerings, and our expectations.

Texture

Here are four observations on the language levels and literary tastes of fourth graders.

1. Fourth graders are conscious of rules. They like to play recess games with complicated codes, they enjoy learning different types of scoring, and they like to keep track of wins and losses. Psychologists tell us this enthusiasm matches the internal work of bringing order to turbulent forces.

Many fourth graders start reading the sports page, with excellent comprehension and reliable memory which makes quick adults feel slow. Recipes and manuals hold new appeal. Reading how to make something takes a new shine.

2. Fourth graders recognize and enjoy more genres of literature than they realize. We can help them capitalize on the width and breadth of their own knowledge through cataloging. Alphabetical order is our tool. Write the alphabet on the board and ask the group to identify one type of literature for each letter. In one ten-minute lesson, I saw a fourth grade class produce the following:

a: almanac
b: biography
c: cartoons
d: description
e: epitaphs
f: fairy tales
g: ghost stories
h: history and humor
i: information
j: jokes
k: kinky lyrics
l: limericks
m: merriment
n: news stories
o: open-ended beginnings
p: poetry
q: questions
r: reporting and riddles
s: stories
t: tirades
u: unexpected twists
v: view descriptions
w: wisecracks

x: either x-rated or excitement
y: yarns
z: zany creatures from zoology

There's nothing sacred about this list, it was born spontaneously among twenty-two children. But it shows the variety most children this age are familiar with. This same teacher pointed out that there are 26 letters in the alphabet, which nearly matches the number of weeks in the school year. He proposed that each week, the class read or write in the genre matching that letter. Of course, some letters have two, three, four or five genres. Some have one or two. That doesn't matter. The students were free to choose among multiple offerings.

3. Fourth graders are old enough to combine words with art, music, and math. They respond well to being shown a picture, whether it be a beautiful print or a scene cut from a magazine, and then being asked to write a description which could serve as the opening setting for a story.

Play a piece of music in the classroom. Ask the students to listen with their eyes closed and "see" who is moving around inside the melody and the rhythm. Then ask them to write a description of that person. The description could be a prose paragraph, a poem, a list of ten comments that person would make, or ten questions and answers the student would invent about the character.

When the teacher explains a mathematical concept, the students should be asked to write it out in prose. This accomplishes two things. First, it checks on comprehension. Second, it joins mathematical and verbal reasoning, opening the way to reading in and about math. Both skills are vital. Students should also be asked (perhaps as homework) to write a math word problem embodying the concept under discussion.

4. Fourth graders are interested in their own development as human beings, and are ready to begin real exploration of the deep, murky, exciting, and dangerous territory of human emotion. Stories which assign human qualities to various animals make a safe entry point. The *Wind In The Willows* offers up hubris, tenderness, loyalty, mockery, gesturing and posturing, humility, and many of the other emotions fourth graders are surprised to discover within themselves. Building an ethical code is easier to do when talking about moles, rats, and badgers than when talking about the kid in the next seat.

Tuck Everlasting and *The Education of Little Tree* are about people and both feed the pool of compassion and complexity.

An adjunct activity is to set out an alphabetical order chart titled "The ABC of the Wonderful Me." Ask the group to find one emotion word for each letter. In fifteen minutes, one fourth grade class produced:

a: anger
b: boredom
c: confusion
d: despair
e: embarrassment
f: frustration
g: gaiety
h: happiness
i: insecurity
j: jealousy
k: kindliness
l: love
m: meanness
n: niceness
o: optimism
p: puzzlement
q: queasiness
r: remorse
s: satisfaction
t: turmoil
u: understanding
v: violence
w: weariness
x: excitement
y: youthfulness
z: zaniness

Once the list is in place, the class can explore synonyms, opposites, and analysis of the optimism or pessimism of the collection. Asked whether there was any emotion on the chart no one had experienced, they all said no. Bringing forth the powerful words which label and describe emotion is a way of legitimizing feelings in the eyes of children, who may fear what they feel inside. The original list can (must) be added to until it overflows the chart. Then each student should take 26 index cards and a notebook ring, and collect his or her own list. This will be a starter tool for launching creative writing, as we will see in Principles of Good Practice.

Structure

Here are five structural elements suitable for fourth graders.

1. Now is the time to take inventory for review, maintenance, or straight teaching of the structural elements referred to in the preceding chapters. They should all be in place.

2. Fourth graders are ready to learn three origins of English words, and assign their vocabularies to the proper categories. (For word lists and detailed explanation, see Marcia Henry's materials, listed in Resources.)

Anglo-Saxon words constitute roughly 15% of our language. Words which are irregular either in reading or spelling, such as "one" or "could," generally belong to this category.

Latin words provide the bulk of our roots and affixes. They follow the rules, and it is easy to figure out their meaning.

Greek words have given us most of our scientific and medical vocabularies, and have specific sound/symbol patterns, such as the *ch* pronounced as /k/, as in school or psyche.

3. Fourth graders who are interested in the rules governing sports and behavior are interested in exceptions to rules in spelling. This is the year to teach "*i* before *e* except after *c* or in 'neither leisured foreigner seized the weird heights'". Other rules and exceptions are listed in *Recipe for Reading* and parallel materials in Resources.

4. Color-coding math words can help students pick their ways through multi-step problems, and can be a boost to those who have trouble remembering which words indicate which process. Take three pieces of poster board. On one, in green ink for growth, write the words which indicate expansion: "sum," "total," "altogether," etc. On the next poster, in red for stop or diminishing, write the words which indicate subtraction or division. On the third, in blue, write the words which indicate ratio. Add to the charts as words come along. I was surprised the first time I saw a student react with panic to a word problem, then

look up at the charts and say, "OK, yeah, 'how much is left?' is a red guy."

5. Handwriting should stabilize this year. Whether it is manuscript, cursive, or D'Neallian doesn't matter. Settling on one and using it consistently does. This is also a developmentally appropriate level to teach correct keyboard fingering, a vital skill for anyone who will be expected to hand in printed materials. That includes everybody these days.

Five Principles of Good Practice

1. Continue the previously begun daily dictation and proofreading exercises outlined in the previous chapter. By now, students are ready to incorporate facts from current events into their dictation, and teachers find this an easy way to solidify names and places in students' minds.

2. Using poster board, make a series of wall charts whose headings are roots and whose body consists of words derived from that root. Keep adding to the corpus. Explain to the students that these are their own words: parts of their vocabulary, their verbal heritage. Once the origin of a word is known, its spelling becomes obvious.

3. Roots Game. Take a piece of poster board and draw a tree with spreading roots, a fat trunk, and leafy branches. Using little pieces of stick-on note paper, write

out a collection of prefixes in green (for go) and suffixes in red (for stop), and sprinkle them around the branches of the tree. On index cards, write root words. Players in turn take a root card, see how many prefixes and suffixes they can affix, earning one point per addition. One fourth grader found to his own amazement that he had made the word "unlovably." Furthermore, he knew the reason for its spelling. By physically manipulating the bits and pieces, the students are putting their hands on the machinery of wordsmithing, and making the gears work. The resultant pleasure keeps them coming back for more.

4. "ABC of the Wonderful Me" writing. Tell the students your initials. Ask them to consult those letters on their notebook ring, choose the letter they think has the most interesting words, and write a story about something they did or saw which flushed up one of the emotions on the card. Many students will have the same letter. Some will have the same emotion, and probably every one will have a different story to go with it. This kind of exercise offers structure, while honoring originality over conformity. When students join experience and emotion with print, they create the fusion which ignites language.

5. Journal Writing. If you are studying a historical period, ask each student to take on the persona of a character from that era and write daily entries about family squabbles, problems of starvation, fire, flood, or exciting events. If you are reading a novel to the students, ask each

one to take a minor character and write a daily journal from that character's point of view. Intersperse opportunities for them to write from their own vantage points, perhaps letting them step into a time warp to be transported to the time of the history lesson or the setting of the fiction.

Fourth graders have the intellectual juggling skills necessary to be themselves and someone else simultaneously. Journal writing and simple reenactments, skits, or short plays allow them to exercise their natural empathy while keeping an intellectual observer's eye on their own thoughts. This is a foundation for later complex thinking which makes the learning of reading, writing, and spelling worth its weight in travail and in triumph.

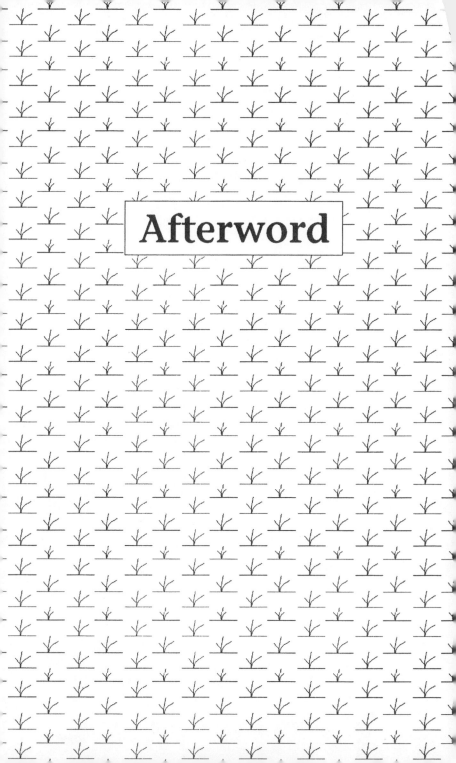

Afterword

Each of us builds and inhabits a house of language. The loveliest are those which rest on strong foundations with footings, cinder blocks, framing, bearing walls, posts and lintels, perhaps a few arches, maybe even a buttress (flying or not), all topped by a roof to keep out weather and a chimney to vent hot air.

But living inside plywood walls in unornamented spaces denies some of our deepest human qualities. From aesthetic longing, the human being has invented windows, shutters, siding, doors, porches and decks, and ways to fill interior spaces with light, shadow, elegance, and simplicity. We have furniture and paintings; we have hooks for heavy coats. We have spaces utilitarian and spaces gracious.

The structure and texture of our linguistic houses sit comfortably on the common ground of whole language and multi-sensory phonics. In fact, the combination may move us to adopt the new phrase "All Language," originally coined by William Ellis, and described in *All Language And The Creation of Literacy* in Resources.

To use well what is outlined in this book, take three steps.

1. See what's already in place. Each school, each grade level, each classroom has its own culture. We want to reinforce what's good, and move toward revision rather than revolution.

2. If the texture and structure of the curriculum is loaded towards "Nan can fan Dan" linguistic readers, or boredom-incarnate basals, we want to move toward liberation by providing nourishment in both receptive and expressive language. If the structure and texture is weighted toward creativity, story telling, drama, and independent reading, we want to be sure the skills have equal billing.

3. We need to monitor the balance between structure and texture throughout the year. One element may be in the ascendancy for a week or two, or a curriculum segment or two. Fine. But then redress. We need to monitor the balance as we consider curriculum planning or revision for forthcoming years, qualifications of teachers being hired, and purchasing decisions.

Educational pendulums swing wide and rhythmically. We keep up with the times by reading, investigating, keeping open minds, and trying new ways gingerly. We need to remember that wide swings of the arc take longer to get back to center. The quick fix is a tempting illusion and a usual flop. "One way" is a sign for traffic, not teaching. Bandwagons boomerang and cults confine. Common ground is a launchpad for common purpose.

Resources

In General

1. The Orton Dyslexia Society, Chester Building, Suite 382, 8600 LaSalle Road, Baltimore, MD, 21204-6020. This organization brings together physicians, researchers, educators, and parents, offering excellent publications and conferences open to any interested participant.

2. Educators Publishing Service, 75 Moulton Street, Cambridge, MA, 02138. This reliable publisher offers materials originally designed for dyslexics which work magnificently in regular classrooms. The descriptions and age/grade levels in their catalogues are scrupulously fair.

3. Modern Learning Press/Programs For Education, Box 167, Rosemont, NJ, 08556. This excellent publishing house offers a wide variety of wholly reliable materials for educators and parents. They are a welcome resource.

Professional Publications

Recipe for Reading. This volume of methods and materials, available from Educator's Publishing Service and based on Orton-Gillingham principles, is a user-friendly companion to classroom teachers.

All Language and the Creation of Literacy. Published by the Orton Dyslexia Society, this compilation of papers shows the interrelationship between structure and texture.

Fraiberg, Selma. *The Magic Years*. New York: Macmillan, 1981. Fraiberg's wisdom gleams like a beacon for parents and anyone else who cares about children.

Henry, Marcia. *Words*. Lex Press, Box 859, Los Gatos, CA, 95031. (See also her books *Tutor 1*, *Tutor 2*, and *Tutor 3*.) Dr. Henry's materials focus on word origins, roots, and affixes. Students enjoy using them; teachers find them clear and successful.

Rosner, Jerome. *Helping Children Overcome Learning Difficulties*. New York: Walker & Co. Rosner's book contains carefully sequenced exercises in auditory segmentation, and blending. Children think they are games; teachers see powerful peripheral growth.

Vail, Neil J. and Joseph F. Papefuss. *Daily Oral Language*. MacDougal, Littell & Co., Box 1667, Evanston, IL 60204. This is a series of statements containing mechanical errors. The teacher writes one on the board, the students must identify the errors, and the teacher makes the corrections.

Vail, Priscilla L. "Watch Out for the Hole in Whole Language." *NY Orton Society Newsletter* and *Independent School*, 1989-90. This is a short article of cautions and concerns.

Vail, Priscilla L. *Clear and Lively Writing: Language Games and Activities for Everyone*. New York: Walker & Co. 1981. This manual of classroom-tested activities and exercises for kids from k-high school offers exercises in the following four categories: listening, reading, speaking, writing.

Vail, Priscilla L. *Smart Kids With School Problems; Things to Know and Ways to Help*. New York: NAL Plume paperback, 1989. In this book, the reader will find clear descriptions and case histories of students with difficulty either in language development or in skill acquisition. The subtitle, "Things to Know and Ways to Help," is self-explanatory.

Vander Molen, Karen and Marilyn Dykema. *Dictation Made Easy*. Van-Dyk Publishers, 2848 Moulford Drive SE, Grand Rapids, MI 49506. This carefully sequenced series of word lists and sentences saves teachers from having to re-invent the wheel.

Zingler, Gary. *At the Pirate Academy: Adventures with Language In the Library Media Center*. Chicago, London: ALA 1990. This new book recounts the experiences of a library/media center teacher and his highly successful ways of bringing focused creativity into all aspects of school life. Practical, original, and humorous, it is an educator's very good friend!

Children's Books

Kindergarten

Curious George by H. Rey

Dr. DeSoto by William Steig

Sylvester & The Magic Pebble by William Steig

A Light in the Attic by Shel Silverstein

Frances by Russell Hoban

A Week of Raccoons by Gloria Whelan

Katy and the Big Snow by Virginia L. Burton

Any of Richard Scarry's books.

First Grade

My Father's Dragon by Ruth Stiles Gannett

Cinderella

The Lion and the Mouse

Puss in Boots

Aladdin and the Magic Lamp

Open Sesame

Miss Rumphius by Barbara Cooney

Mac and Tab (The first in a series of small, paperback phonic readers available from Educators Publishing Service.)

Second Grade

The Magic Schoolbus by Joanna Cole

Mio, My Son by Astrid Lindgren

Pippi Longstocking by Astrid Lindgren

Matilda by Roald Dahl

Cautionary Verses by Hilaire Belloc

Our Animal Friends at Maple Hill Farm by M. & A. Provenson

Amelia Bedelia by Peggy Parish

Third Grade

Ramona by Beverly Cleary

The King Who Rained by Fred Gwynne

In The Beginning by Virginia Hamilton

Norse Gods & Giants by Ingri & Edgar Parin D'Aulaire

Greek Myths by Ingri & Edgar Parin D'Aulaire

Where the Wild Things Are by Maurice Sendak

Maggie B. by Irene Haas

Brave Irene by William Steig

The Story of Jumping Mouse by John Steptoe

Wrinkle in Time by Madelaine L'Engle

The Bad Island by William Steig

Fourth Grade

The Wind in the Willows by Kenneth Grahame

Tuck Everlasting by Natalie Babbit

The Education of Little Tree by Forrest Carter

Other Books by Priscilla Vail
Available from Modern Learning Press

The World of the Gifted Child

Clear and Lively Writing

Gifted, Precocious or Just Plain Smart

Smart Kids with School Problems

About Dyslexia

For more information, contact
Modern Learning Press
P.O. Box 167
Rosemont, NJ 08556

or call toll-free
1-800-627-5867